GW00854134

FINANCIAL M
NATIONAL ECONOMIES

William A. Allen

THE ROYAL INSTITUTE OF
INTERNATIONAL AFFAIRS
International Economics Programme

Published in Great Britain in 2001
by the Royal Institute of International Affairs,
Chatham House, 10 St James's Square, London SW1Y 4LE
(Charity Registration No. 208 223)

Distributed worldwide by the Brookings Institution,
1775 Massachusetts Avenue, NW, Washington, DC 20036-2188

ISBN 1 86203 130 4

Cover design by Matthew Link
Cover image shows the booby, a significant contributor to the world
trade in guano.
Printed and bound in Great Britain by the Chameleon Press Ltd

CONTENTS

FOREWORD

Financial turmoil in the 1980s and 1990s encouraged the belief that international monetary relations had changed either because of increasing and freer capital flows or as the result of bad exchange rate management, or both. Some observers take for granted that increasing capital flows were at fault and conclude that capital controls are necessary. Others conclude that the fault lies with bad exchange rate management rather than capital movements.

William Allen takes the line that capital is still far from completely mobile internationally, and considerably less mobile than in the nineteenth and early twentieth centuries when capital flew from Paris and London to finance everything from American and Russian railways to Peruvian guano. He then examines the remaining obstacles to complete mobility. The paper focuses on exchange rate issues and discusses the options facing monetary authorities in the context of current financial market conditions. These issues remain contentious, and the paper suggests that the choice among the various options depends on the constantly evolving micro-economic nature of the foreign exchange market.

This paper is a pleasure to read not only because it is so lucidly written but mainly because William Allen does not take for granted a single concept in the changing nature of international monetary relations over the past forty years; each point is argued thoroughly. In this sense, William Allen has shown not only that he belongs to the highest tradition of civil servants but that he is a true scholar. I am proud to publish it as part of the International Economics Programme's contribution to current and topical debate on the International Financial Architecture.

Dr Brigitte Granville
Head, International Economics Programme
Royal Institute of International Affairs

ABOUT THE AUTHOR

William A. Allen is a Deputy Director of the Bank of England. He is responsible for the central bank's dealing operations in financial markets, and for its Centre for Central Banking Studies, which organizes dialogue on central banking issues and provides training and technical assistance to emerging country central banks. Educated at Oxford University and the London School of Economics, he has worked at the Bank of England since 1972.

ACKNOWLEDGMENTS

This paper is based on a lecture delivered to the RIIA International Economics Programme seminar on 12 October 2000. I am grateful to the distinguished participants in the seminar, and to Peter Andrews, Neal Hatch, Richhild Moessner, Adrian Penalver and Clifford Smout, for their comments on it. Above all, I am grateful to Brigitte Granville, for stimulating and thought-provoking advice on how to turn the lecture into a paper. The paper does not reflect the views of the Bank of England.

W.A.A.

EXECUTIVE SUMMARY

This paper is about the interrelationship between international financial markets and national economic management. The importance of the relationship is obvious, in the light of the continuing frequent incidence of financial crises in individual countries. The paper begins with an assessment of the performance of financial markets in one of their main international functions – the international allocation of savings to productive investment opportunities, and how their performance has evolved in the light of developments over the past forty years, including the liberalization of international trade and investment and the growth of the financial intermediation industry.

The paper goes on to consider what are the remaining obstacles to market efficiency in the international arena. Those obstacles include official controls on capital flows, cultural and legal factors, and fears of monetary and financial instability. The paper focuses on exchange rate issues and discusses the options facing monetary authorities in the context of current financial market conditions. These issues remain contentious, even though they have been debated for many decades, and the paper suggests that the choice among the various options depends on the microeconomic nature of the foreign exchange market, which has tended to change from time to time and will continue to change.

1 THE FUNCTIONING OF
INTERNATIONAL FINANCIAL MARKETS

One of the principal functions of financial markets is to allocate savings efficiently to finance investment opportunities. Indeed, this is a large part of the justification for the existence of financial markets. In principle, if markets work efficiently, the most productive investment opportunities will be financed and this will help to maximize the returns to new investment and the rate of economic growth.[1]

In 1980 two economists, Martin Feldstein and Charles Horioka, published an article which measured the international mobility of capital.[2] They hypothesized that in a world of capital mobility, the location of the most productive investment opportunities would be unrelated to the location of large amounts of savings. Thus there should be no correlation between a cross-section of national domestic investment ratios (domestic investment relative to GDP) and domestic savings ratios (domestic savings relative to GDP). Countries in which domestic savings exceeded domestic investment would invest the surplus in other countries; and countries in which domestic investment exceeded domestic savings

[1] See P. Brenton, H. Scott and P. Sinclair, *International Trade* (Oxford: Oxford University Press, 1997).
[2] M. Feldstein and C. Horioka, 'Domestic saving and international capital flows', *Economic Journal*, Vol. 90, June 1980, pp. 314–29.

would use the surplus savings of countries in the former group. Examining data from OECD countries over the period 1960–74, they found that, contrary to this hypothesis, there was a strong correlation between national savings and investment ratios. They concluded that capital was far from perfectly mobile internationally.

It is worth devoting a little time to discussing the assumption on which Feldstein and Horioka based their conclusion. Is it realistic to assume that the location of the most productive investment opportunities is unrelated to the location of high savings ratios? Two possible reasons for expecting that they might be related in some way are:

(i) High savings rates may be associated with a relatively low level of state welfare provision, which is in turn likely to be associated with relatively low taxation. Low taxation is likely to attract investment.

(ii) The statistical evidence is that high savings rates are associated with relatively high per capita incomes. Relatively high per capita incomes are likely in turn to be associated with a relatively high cost of labour – which is likely to repel labour-using investment, though it might encourage labour-saving investment.

These considerations have diverse implications for the expected correlation between savings and investment ratios: it is not clear how significant they are or which is likely to dominate. In the absence of further information, it seems reasonable to suppose that if capital were perfectly mobile internationally, then the correlation between national savings and investment ratios would be pretty small.

The twenty years since Feldstein and Horioka published their paper have been a period of remarkably fast growth in financial markets. It is of interest to look at the evidence again, to see whether the mobility of capital has increased.[3] I have used data from 29 OECD countries, since they are readily available. The data extend from 1960 to 1997, and encompass a widening range of countries. South Korea is included from 1970, the Czech Republic, Hungary and Poland from 1990. West Germany turns into Germany in 1991. The details of the calculation are set out in the appendix.

The results are most conveniently summarized by one figure for each decade, representing the cross-country correlation coefficient between national savings and investment ratios over that decade. The figure must be less than one: the closer it is to zero, the less closely correlated are national savings and investment ratios and the more internationally mobile is capital. At the other extreme, a correlation coefficient approaching one would show that national savings and investment ratios were very closely correlated and that international capital was not very mobile. The results are shown in Table 1.

The results suggest that there has been a trend towards increasing international capital mobility. However, they probably exaggerate the level of international capital mobility. In each of the four decades I looked at, the country with the largest difference between domestic

[3] The G10 study of 1995 on 'Savings, Investment and Real Interest Rates' explored the influences of global savings and investment on global real interest rates, assuming an integrated world capital market.

Table 1: Correlation coefficients between national savings and investment ratios

Period	Correlation coefficient
1960–69	0.83
1970–79	0.56
1980–89	0.71
1990–97	0.62

investment and domestic saving was Greece. In the 1960s and 1970s, investment exceeded saving by more than 11% of GDP. Almost certainly, in Greece's case, the excess was financed largely by international transfers, including remittances from Greek citizens working abroad, rather than by international flows of investment funds.[4] Ireland also had a large excess of investment over domestic savings in the 1960s and 1970s, and this may well have been financed largely by transfers from Irish citizens working abroad. But Ireland's spectacular economic growth has turned the position completely around, so that between 1990 and 1997, Irish domestic savings exceeded investment by over 10% of GDP.

It is not surprising that capital mobility has increased since the 1960s. For one thing, there has been a widespread retreat from the use of capital controls as a weapon of economic policy (though some countries have returned

[4] If Greece is excluded from the data, the correlations between savings and investment rates are rather higher, particularly in the 1960s and 1970s: 1960s 0.91; 1970s 0.66; 1980s 0.76; 1990s 0.66.

to capital controls in the past few years).[5] And Richard Baldwin and Philippe Martin have suggested that the increased ease, reliability and lower cost of telecommunications have stimulated foreign direct investment;[6] they seem likely to have stimulated other forms of international investment as well. It is perhaps surprising that the increase in capital mobility appears to have been unsteady, with a sharp increase between the 1960s and the 1970s, followed by a relapse in the 1980s and a modest recovery in the 1990s. The apparent increase in capital mobility in the 1970s may well reflect the huge OPEC external surpluses and the counterpart deficits in industrial countries, which may have shown up in weakened correlations between national savings and investment ratios in OECD countries. But the 1970s were an eventful decade and other developments will also have been influential.

Other studies,[7] while supporting the conclusion that capital has been somewhat more mobile internationally since the 1960s, suggest that international capital was at its most mobile in the period from 1860 to 1914 and in the 1920s, and that it has not thus far recaptured the mobility which it displayed then.

[5] See Jeffrey R. Shafer, 'Experience with controls on international capital movements in OECD countries: solution or problem for monetary policy?', in Sebastian Edwards (ed.), *Capital Controls, Exchange Rates and Monetary Policy in the World Economy* (Cambridge: Cambridge University Press, 1995).
[6] Richard E. Baldwin and Philippe Martin, *Two Waves of Globalisation: Superficial Similarities, Fundamental Differences*, NBER Working Paper 6904, January 1999.
[7] For example, Alan M. Taylor, *International Capital Mobility in History: The Saving–Investment Relationship*, NBER Working Paper 5743, September 1996.

5

Very recently, the widening gap between investment and savings in the United States may be regarded as evidence of international capital mobility – at least *into* the United States. The gap has widened steadily since the mid-1990s and was up to 3.3% of US GDP in the first half of 2000. This gap is much larger than the gap between the investment and savings ratios in the United States when it was industrializing rapidly between 1874 and 1913, according to the data quoted by Taylor.[8] Countries with sustained shortfalls of savings relative to investment of this scale relative to GDP over a decade in the period since 1960 have generally been countries which have large numbers of expatriate workers in western Europe remitting part of their earnings to their native country (such as Greece, Ireland, Portugal and Turkey). However, South Korea had a shortfall of savings relative to investment of 6% of GDP in the 1970s.

[8] Ibid.

2 WHAT ARE THE OBSTACLES TO INTERNATIONAL MOBILITY OF CAPITAL?

In the light of this empirical result it makes sense to consider the obstacles to greater international mobility of capital. I plan to group them into three categories, but to discuss only one of the categories in much depth.

(a) Official controls on capital flows

The first category of possible obstacles is *official controls on capital flows*. Traditionally, countries placed controls on outflows of capital – for example, the United Kingdom did so for 40 years, from 1939 to 1979. The controls might have been expected to trap domestic savings within national boundaries and thereby reduce the required rate of return on domestic investment, and to stimulate domestic investment at the expense of investment in the rest of the world. Experience in the United Kingdom and elsewhere did not suggest that the controls that were in operation succeeded in achieving this intended objective. Nor did they succeed in protecting the United Kingdom from currency crises during that period. In a general review of capital controls, Sebastian Edwards[9] concludes that 'the existing historical evidence suggests quite sharply that controls on outflows – and, in

[9] Sebastian Edwards, 'How Effective are Capital Controls?', *Journal of Economic Perspectives*, Vol. 13, No. 4, Fall 1999.

particular, quantitative controls on outflows – have been largely ineffective'. The desirability of capital controls began to be questioned in the 1960s and there ensued a very gradual movement away from capital controls in OECD countries – a process described in detail by Shafer.[10] And of course the collapse of the Soviet Union and the liberation of its former satellites in Central and Eastern Europe has brought with it a massive liberalization of controls on international capital flows into and out of those countries.

More recently, in the light of financial crises in many emerging countries during the 1990s, there has been a renewed debate about the desirability and utility of capital controls as an economic policy weapon.[11] It has become widely accepted that care needs to be taken in the sequencing of financial liberalization measures,[12] because premature liberalization can have destabilizing effects, if it takes place, say, before domestic banking systems have developed the skills and infrastructure needed to intermediate between international lenders and domestic borrowers. Indeed, premature liberalization in many countries is widely believed to have contributed to the Asian currency crisis of 1997–8. Some

[10] Shafer, 'Experience with Controls' (see note 5 above).
[11] See, for example, Christine P. Ries and Richard J. Sweeney (eds), *Capital Controls in Emerging Economies* (Boulder, CO: Westview Press, 1997); Richard N. Cooper, 'Should Capital Controls be Banished?', *Brookings Papers on Economic Activity*, 1:1999; Edwards, 'How Effective are Capital Controls?'.
[12] See Barry Eichengreen, Michael Mussa et al., *Capital Account Liberalisation: Theoretical and Practical Aspects*, International Monetary Fund, 1998.

countries have placed restrictions on capital flows, particularly short-term capital inflows, in order to reduce the risk of volatile short-term capital flows causing instability in the domestic economy. Chile was a pioneer in this.[13] Malaysia responded to the Asian currency crisis by imposing extensive capital controls, though they have now been partly relaxed. Many other emerging countries maintain some controls on capital flows: typically the controls are concentrated on short-term flows rather than direct investment and longer-term flows. Those countries wishing to join the European Union will be obliged to withdraw the controls as a condition of membership.

It seems to be widely recognized in the debate that controls on inflows are likely to be more effective than controls on outflows, because those wishing to move investment funds into a particular country normally have a wide range of alternatives, i.e. investing in other countries, whereas those wishing to move investment funds out of a particular country have only one alternative, i.e. leaving the funds in that country.[14] Nevertheless, inflow controls have the drawback that they deny the country in question access to funds that might otherwise contribute to economic development.

To summarize, capital controls remain in some countries, but they are much less pervasive than in the 1960s

[13] For an appraisal of recent Chilean capital controls, see F. Gallego, L. Hernandez and K. Schmidt-Hebbel, 'Capital Controls in Chile: Effective? Efficient?', *Central Bank of Chile Working Papers*, No. 59, December 1999.
[14] The book cited in note 11 surveys empirical evidence that inflow controls have been more effective than outflow controls.

and 1970s and they are mainly aimed at short-term flows. The move away from capital controls over the past twenty years has probably been one of the reasons why the correlation between national savings and investment rates has declined. Does a 'new wave' of capital controls threaten international capital mobility? Although capital controls have come back into fashion in the past few years, as noted above, the new controls introduced in this period have generally been intended to provide protection against monetary and financial instability, which is one of the other main obstacles to international capital mobility discussed in this paper. If, but only if, the 'new wave' of capital controls succeeds in keeping monetary and financial instability at bay, then it can be positive rather than negative for international capital mobility.

(b) Cultural and legal factors

In his survey of economic growth in the past millennium, David Landes comments that 'if we learn anything from the history of economic development, it is that culture makes all the difference'.[15] And Francis Fukuyama[16] holds out the prospect that continuing scientific advances will lead inescapably to a kind of global cultural and economic unification. I do not plan to discuss these great issues in any depth, but just to make a couple of rather obvious points about cultural and legal obstacles to international investment.

[15] David S. Landes, *The Wealth and Poverty of Nations* (London: Little, Brown & Co, 1998), p. 516.
[16] Francis Fukuyama, *The End of History and the Last Man* (Harmondsworth: Penguin Books, 1992).

One possible obstacle is simple ignorance of the prospective host country. It is not realistic to think that, for example, investment by big multinational oil companies is inhibited in any way by ignorance of any part of the world that is potentially relevant to their industry. This is partly because these companies are big themselves and contemplate investments which are big enough to warrant extensive and expensive research, and partly because the information which matters most to them relates to a particular industry. But it is reasonable to think that portfolio investors and bank lenders are held back in some cases by lack of information about countries in which they might invest. This may be partly because the countries simply do not make the inform- ation available, but in some cases it could also be that the country concerned is too small or too economically insignificant for it to be in the private interests of anyone in the private sector to analyse its economy, to monitor its progress and development and to become generally familiar with it.[17] It could be argued that this represents a 'market failure' and that in the global interest, the function of economic analysis should be performed, and the results published, by a publicly funded institu- tion: it is an issue on which reasonable people can and do have different views.

Leaving simple ignorance aside, it is fairly clear that one of the factors which bear heavily on investment

[17] Investors often talk about the need to 'feel comfortable' with a deal. The language perhaps suggests that they want something more than cold information, and that the familiarity which comes from travel, social relationships and the memory of previous dealings is of great value.

11

decisions by international companies is the state of the law in the prospective host country, particularly on issues such as labour relations and enforcement of commercial claims. The desire to attract foreign direct investment thus creates pressure on host countries to adapt their laws and practices to make them more attractive to international investors. That can create tension between domestic cultural and sometimes also religious sentiment, and the interests of 'globalization'. Perhaps in the past twenty years the benefits of direct investment have become more readily apparent, and national legislatures and governments have increasingly been prepared to adapt themselves to attract it. The economic benefits of inward investment come not just in the form of higher private incomes but also in the form of better public services and public amenities financed by higher tax receipts. It is also true that the benefits are often unequally distributed, and that they often widen existing inequalities in host countries.

Of course, the economic benefits are likely to have cultural consequences. Whether those are beneficial or damaging is, however, likely to be a matter of dispute: they can be applauded as 'progress' or stigmatized as 'cultural imperialism' according to taste. The issue is whether the economic benefits prove to be large enough, and whether they materialize quickly enough, to compensate for any widening of inequalities which they entail and for the loss of cultural specialness and identity which is necessary to secure them. This is an issue to be resolved country by country and perhaps region by region. Views on it change over time and recently have been changing in the direction of greater engagement with the world economy. China's keenness to be admitted to the World Trade Organization is striking evidence of this. Nevertheless, there is no reason why any country should be forced to participate in the international economy against its will. For the purposes of this paper, it is sufficient to note that the effect of globalization on national culture is a deep issue which is capable of obstructing the international flow of capital.[18]

One important current issue, which perhaps falls into this broad cultural/legal category, is the so-called 'Washington consensus' on economic management. The Washington consensus represents the view of what might be called the international economics establishment on how countries should best manage their economic and financial affairs. It embraces not only macroeconomic policy but also matters such as official supervision of financial institutions and financial markets and the proper relationship between the public sector and the private sector. It has been further developed and proselytized with much more vigour in the light of an examination of 'what went wrong' in the Mexican crisis of 1994–5 and the Asian crisis of 1997–8, in which industrialized countries felt obliged to put large amounts of public money at stake to prevent serious damage to the world economy, and of the perception that a large part of 'what went wrong' was bad policies in the countries that were hit by the crisis.

[18] Sylvia Ostry ('Globalisation and Sovereignty', J. R. Malory Annual Lecture, 1998, McGill Institute for the Study of Canada, available at *http://www.arts.mcgill.ca/programms/misc/ostry.htm*) describes the political forces which have promoted global economic integration and how they have affected political developments within Canada.

The Washington consensus is manifested in 'codes' and 'standards' for the conduct of various aspects of public economic and financial policy. For example, the IMF has developed three standards – on data dissemination, fiscal transparency, and transparency in monetary and financial policies; and the Financial Stability Forum has also been extremely active in promulgating standards – 66 of them are listed on its website.

These codes and standards have not come out of thin air. They represent best practice as it is currently understood, based in many cases on the hard experiences of those who have in the past not always followed best practice, for example in exchange rate management. In other words, they represent good advice. Nevertheless they have engendered a great deal of resistance from some of the countries for whose benefit they are intended. One reason is the ever-present suspicion that adherence to some or all of the codes and standards will become a new and additional condition for access to financial assistance from the IMF. A second reason is the assertion that, despite the rhetoric, they are really being put forward in the interests of the developed countries. Another, related, reason is the perception that they are infringing national sovereignty in economic and financial management; and that adherence to them requires resources, in the form of highly trained people (such as banking supervisors), in quantities which are far beyond the means of poorer countries. A fourth reason is that adherence to them might threaten bureaucratic interests in the countries in question, even if it would be in the interests of the country as a whole. Yet another reason is doubts about the usefulness of the advice. It is regrettable but undeniable that the causes of economic growth are not fully understood, and many countries (such as South Korea in the 1960s and 1970s) have enjoyed periods of spectacular economic growth while pursuing extremely politically incorrect economic policies.[19] And, to quote Joseph Stiglitz, the former Chief Economist of the World Bank,

> It is clear that the prescriptions which came to be called the Washington Consensus are not sufficient for development, since many countries that followed the precepts have still failed to achieve even moderate levels of growth.[20]

The Washington consensus does not and cannot contain the elixir of economic growth. Even so, it contains a great deal of very useful advice.

(c) Monetary and financial instability

This third category of obstacles to international investment is the one to which this paper will devote the most attention. It can be loosely described as the concern that something will go badly wrong with the monetary or financial system of the host country and that, as a result, the assumptions on which international investment decisions were based will be falsified, to the investor's cost. There have been many such episodes in financial

[19] In the early 1970s, the late Professor Harry Johnson once remarked that 'growth economics' merely describes what happens when economic growth occurs; it does not explain why economic growth occurs.
[20] 'The World Bank at the Millennium', *Economic Journal*, Vol. 109, November 1999, pp. 577–97.

Table 2: Percentage falls in real GDP and private consumer spending in crisis-hit economies

	Year	Percentage change in real GDP	Percentage change in private consumer spending
Mexico	1995	−6.2	−10.2
Hong Kong	1998	−5.1	−6.5
Indonesia	1998	−13.2	−3.3
Malaysia	1998	−7.4	−12.3
Russia	1998	−4.9	−8.2
South Korea	1998	−6.7	−8.7
Thailand	1998	−10.2	−9.5

Sources: IMF, *International Financial Statistics;* Bank Indonesia, *Annual Report 1999.*

history – for example in many industrial countries, including the UK in the 1970s; Mexico in 1994–5; several Asian countries in 1997; Russia in 1998. Of course, these episodes are often unhappy ones not only for international investors but also for the host country itself, which in many cases finds itself obliged to endure a massive and sudden contraction in living standards as a result of a financial crisis. The common feature of these episodes is that they involve large actual or threatened changes in exchange rates, and that assumptions and beliefs which investors have hitherto regarded as axiomatic are suddenly called into question and often overturned.

Table 2 shows how real GDP and private consumer spending have contracted in economies which have been afflicted by financial crises.

In the light of the effects of financial crises on living standards, it is not surprising that the debate on how monetary and exchange rate policies should best be conducted continues to attract close attention. For decades there has been a debate about exchange rate management and the relative merits of fixed and floating rates: that debate remains unsettled. Chapter 3 comments on the debate, and discusses how countries can best protect themselves against the risks of externally induced monetary instability.

3 THE DEBATE ON EXCHANGE RATE MANAGEMENT

Countries have a range of options in managing their monetary affairs. The options they have chosen in practice have depended partly on their own national circumstances, but also on the prevailing conditions in the foreign exchange market. This chapter traces the ways in which changing microeconomic conditions in the foreign exchange market have affected the debate and discusses how recent microeconomic changes may affect it in the future. It begins by describing the options, and then goes on to discuss how they interact with the microeconomics of the foreign exchange market.

(a) Options for exchange rate management

(i) Dollarization

Starting at the most rigid end of the spectrum, one option is to use someone else's currency – an option currently known as 'dollarization'. Panama has dollarized, for example,[21] and Ecuador has now done so as well. In addition, the US dollar is widely used informally in Russia, in Africa and in Latin America in particular, even though there are official local currencies. The dollar is a

[21] See Kurt A. Schuler, 'Currency Boards', PhD dissertation, George Mason University, Fairfax, Virginia, 1992; available at *http://users.erols.com/kurrency/webdiss1.htm*.

popular choice in places where the official local currency is unsatisfactory for whatever reason: dollarization can take place unofficially (though the state can insist that transactions with itself are conducted in local currency). The banknote circulation of the United States amounts to around $2,000 per head of population of the USA – or, to put it another way, around $100 per head of population in the entire world (see Table 3). It has been estimated that over 50% by value of dollar bills were located outside the United States as at the end of 1995.[22] No other currency can compare. For example, Deutschmark banknotes, like dollar bills, are extensively used outside their country of origin, notably in the Balkans: Montenegro has adopted the Deutschmark as its official currency. The total circulation of DM banknotes amounts to about $1,500 per head of German population, though that is only about $20 per head of world population. It will be extremely interesting to see what happens to this external demand for banknotes when they are replaced by euro notes in 2002. The UK banknote circulation amounts to roughly $700 per head of UK population, but just $7 per head of world population.[23] Hoarding of dollar (and Deutschmark) bills was

[22] See Richard D. Porter and Ruth A. Judson, 'The Location of US Currency: How Much Is Abroad?', *Federal Reserve Bulletin*, October 1996.
[23] The amount of yen banknotes outstanding is extremely large – $4,000 per head of Japan's population, or $90 per head of world population. Yet there are few, if any, reports of the yen being used as an international currency. There are three reasons why a very large domestic circulation of banknotes in Japan would not be surprising: first, Japanese interest rates are extremely low, so that the opportunity cost of holding banknotes is minimal; second, the Japanese public may have residual concerns about the soundness of

19

Table 3: Banknote circulation per head of national and world population, 2000 ($)

Currency	Banknote circulation per head of national population	Banknote circulation per head of world population
US dollar	2,000	100
Deutschmark*	1,500	20
Pound sterling	700	7

* The Deutschmark has since 1999 been a non-decimal denomination of the euro – but until 2002 there are no euro banknotes, and DM banknotes remain in circulation.
Source: National central banks.

a widespread practice in the former communist countries of Central and Eastern Europe, and the monetary authorities of their post-communist administrations often measure their success in rehabilitating their national currencies by measuring how far the degree of dollarization of the economy has fallen.

A variant of 'using someone else's currency' is joining a monetary union, like the twelve member countries of the European Union which have adopted the single

commercial banks and therefore a preference for banknotes; and, third, the incidence of crime in Japan is low, so that the risk that banknotes will be stolen is not very great. Likewise, a very large amount of Swiss franc banknotes per head of domestic population is also outstanding – $2,400. As in the case of Japan, this probably partly reflects domestic influences: low interest rates and low incidence of crime. Moreover, Swiss payment techniques are unusually banknote-intensive. There are few reports of international use of Swiss banknotes for transaction purposes, however, and the Swiss franc banknote circulation amounts to only $3 per head of world population.

currency, or like the members of the CFA Franc zone. Joining a monetary union is analytically the same as 'using someone else's currency' but with the very important difference that the currency of the monetary union is managed in the interests of the entire currency area – whereas the dollar, for example, is managed exclusively in the interests of the USA. Of course, I recognize that the European single currency has enormous political significance in addition to its economic implications, but that is not the subject of this paper.

(ii) Currency board

Another option at the rigid end of the spectrum is a currency board. A currency board issues banknotes, which have to be backed one-for-one by holdings of safe assets denominated in the reserve currency. Holdings of local currency can be exchanged freely for the reserve currency at par. In a sense, the classical gold standard which operated in the United Kingdom after the Bank Charter Act of 1844 was a currency board: the Bank of England was authorized to issue banknotes but they had to be backed by holdings of gold, which played the role of the reserve currency. Later many British colonies operated currency boards, and issued local currency notes which were backed one-for-one by holdings of sterling, which was usually invested in UK Treasury bills. The exchange rate against sterling was thus fixed. Compared with simply using sterling as the local currency, a currency board had two advantages. First, the local economy got the benefit of the seigniorage on the currency – that is, it received the interest income on the Treasury bills in which the currency board's assets were invested. If the colony had simply used sterling as its local currency, the British government would have got the benefit of the seigniorage. Second, and more mundanely, banknotes could be printed locally, so that the transport costs of delivering new notes to replace worn-out ones were much lower.

Much more recently still, several countries or territories have introduced currency boards as a means of building or restoring confidence in their currencies. Examples include Hong Kong, Argentina, Bulgaria and Estonia. One important but under-recognized feature of currency boards is that they can be effectively dissolved without the need for any formalities if the public demand for the currency in question falls away. The public could simply exchange the local currency for the reserve currency at par, under the rules of the currency board. The board's assets and liabilities would decline in parallel, and in the extreme the local currency will simply disappear. The consumer is king. In practice, however, as far as I know no currency board has ever disappeared in this way.[24]

A common feature of both dollarization and currency board arrangements is that the public authorities do not have the unlimited power to create new money, because of the requirement for one-for-one backing by holdings of the reserve currency. This can be a severe constraint on fiscal policy, and on the ability of the monetary authorities to arrange emergency support for financial institutions

[24] Schuler, in 'Currency Boards' (note 21 above), describes the historical circumstances and the ways in which currency boards have been dissolved.

in difficulty. There are a number of methods of easing the severity of the constraint. One is for the monetary authority to hold excess reserves, beyond what are needed to support the domestic currency in issue, so that the surplus can be used in emergencies. A second is for the monetary authorities to arrange borrowing facilities from either public or private sources which can be activated unconditionally in case of need. The IMF's contingent credit facility is intended for this purpose. A third – resorted to from time to time in the United Kingdom during the gold standard period – is simply to suspend the rules for a period. However, even though these expedients are available, the concern that emergency official support, if needed, might be constrained by a shortage of funds probably represents a competitive disadvantage to commercial banks domiciled in currency board countries.[25]

(iii) 'Fixed but adjustable' exchange rates

Moving one stage further along the spectrum, the next option is so-called 'fixed but adjustable' exchange rates. This was the exchange rate regime embodied in the Bretton Woods structure, and in the European Exchange Rate Mechanism. It was introduced into the former in reaction to what was then perceived as disorderly experience with floating exchange rates in the 1930s, which was

[25] Veerathai Santiprabhob, in 'Bank Soundness and Currency Board Arrangements: Issues and Experience', *IMF Paper on Policy Analysis and Assessment*, December 1997, describes ways in which monetary authorities in currency board countries can ameliorate the effects of the constraint.

thought to have inhibited the recovery of international trade and economic activity during that turbulent decade. The idea is to minimize the scope for uncertainty about the exchange rate by announcing a parity, and a band either side of the parity within which the exchange rate is allowed to fluctuate. It is, however, recognized that economic developments, such as, for example, differential rates of inflation, can render a previously declared parity obsolete and unsustainable, so that there is a so-called 'fundamental disequilibrium'. In those circumstances, the parity can be changed by agreement among the parties to the arrangement.

Not all fixed-but-adjustable exchange rate regimes are the subject of international agreements. Many countries peg their currencies unilaterally to another currency or to a basket of currencies, but maintain the ability to adjust the peg at their own discretion.

Some variations are possible within this general framework. For example, the width of the fluctuation bands can be varied. In the Bretton Woods structure, the fluctuation bands were 1% either side of parity against the US dollar. The European Exchange Rate Mechanism began life in 1972 as a European successor to the recently deceased Bretton Woods system. The exchange rate arrangements in the ERM were slightly more complicated but the maximum range of fluctuation between any two member currencies was $2^{1}/_{4}\%$, though it was possible to join with a wider band of 6%. After the crisis of 1992–3 the band widths increased to 15%.

Another variation is in the degree of tenacity with which countries maintain their parity under market pressure, or, to put it another way, how ready they are to declare that there is a 'fundamental disequilibrium' and change the exchange rate parity. There are often powerful forces resisting a change in parity. For example, a revaluation is likely to be resisted by exporters and other producers of internationally tradable goods and services; and it is likely to threaten increased unemployment, at least in the short term. Devaluation is often politically humiliating and may be regarded as threatening high or at least higher inflation, and a loss of monetary policy credibility. And where parity changes require international agreement, the necessary negotiations are not straightforward if partner countries think that the proposed parity change threatens their interests or if they want to trade off agreement on the proposed parity change against concessions on some other issue.

(iv) Floating exchange rates

As the fluctuation bands widen, and as the tenacity with which parities are defended decreases, fixed-but-adjustable exchange rate regimes transmute into floating regimes. Even within the floating category there are variants. For example, even if the monetary authorities do not intervene in the foreign exchange market by buying or selling their own currency, they may nevertheless express, in words, their views about the appropriate level of the exchange rate (this practice is sometimes called 'open-mouth policy', to distinguish it from open-market policy, which involves actually dealing in the market). And occasionally, even if they have a floating exchange rate, they may accompany words by intervention (open-market policy) intended to move the exchange rate in the direction they consider appropriate. This may be by international agreement – such as the Plaza agreement to sell dollars in 1985 or the G7 agreement to buy euros in September 2000. Or it may be a unilateral enterprise, as with much of the intervention conducted by Japan to manage the exchange rate of the yen (in both directions) since 1995.

Some countries intervene in the foreign exchange market very rarely indeed – Switzerland, for example. But as far as I am aware, in no country with a floating exchange rate is it impossible or illegal for the central bank to intervene in the foreign exchange market.

In the long-running debate about fixed and floating exchange rates, the leading issue has rightly been the value that should be attached to the monetary policy autonomy that a floating exchange rate allows but a fixed exchange rate denies.[26] Casual observation reveals that, on the whole, large countries tend to have floating exchange rates while small countries have fixed ones. One reason is easy to understand: a large country is more likely than a small one to have a well-diversified and relatively closed economy. In the jargon of economics, the shocks, or unexpected developments, to which a large country has to react are likely to be largely idiosyncratic, and since other countries are unlikely to have experienced the same shocks, exchange rate flexibility is likely to be useful in helping to react to them. In a small

[26] Capital controls, if they are effective, can be a means of retaining some monetary policy autonomy while maintaining a fixed exchange rate. They are discussed in Chapter 2 above.

country, economic shocks are more likely to be experiences shared with neighbouring countries, and an exchange rate which can vary against neighbouring currencies will not help much in responding to them. This view is derived from the theory of optimal currency areas put forward by Robert Mundell.[27]

In practice, the most difficult questions about choice of exchange rate regime are those faced by countries which are neither very small, like Luxembourg, nor very large, like the United States. They don't really know, and economists can't tell them with any conviction, whether they constitute an optimal currency area on their own or whether the optimal currency area extends beyond their boundaries. For these countries, the choice of exchange rate regime is a difficult one, and I want to suggest that the microeconomic nature of the foreign exchange market is a relevant consideration in making the choice.

(b) The microeconomic nature of the foreign exchange market

I should first make clear what I mean by the microeconomic nature of the foreign exchange market, and I will do so by reviewing the historical evolution of the market. In the thirty years or so up to, say, 1980, there were quite extensive controls on international flows of investment capital, as noted above. The controls were generally concentrated on short-term flows, which would probably, had they not been controlled, have accounted

[27] R. A. Mundell, 'A Theory of Optimum Currency Areas', *American Economic Review*, Vol. 51, November 1961, pp. 509–17.

for the largest share of market turnover. Therefore trade and long-term investment flows, together with interest and profit remittances and international transfers, accounted for a much larger share of foreign exchange market turnover at that time than they did later. The distinguishing feature of these flows is that, in the short term, they are not related very closely to the fundamental economic determinants of exchange rates. I do not mean to suggest that short-term capital flows were completely suppressed. Capital controls could have completely suppressed them only at the cost of crippling international trade. In particular, importers and exporters had to be allowed some flexibility over the timing of their payments and receipts. Not surprisingly, when a devaluation was expected, payments for imports were accelerated and receipts for exports were delayed. The result was the equivalent of a short-term capital outflow. Nevertheless, capital controls did seriously inhibit short-term capital flows and position-taking based on views of foreign exchange market fundamentals.

Nor do I mean to suggest that exchange rates in this period were therefore unaffected by fundamentals: it is obvious, for example, that a country with an overvalued exchange rate would over time develop a deficit on trade and long-term investment flows, leading to excess supply of its currency and market pressure for the exchange rate to depreciate. The point is rather that it could take quite a long time for the fundamentals to bear on the market.

This meant, among other things, that monetary authorities had plenty of time to reflect before making parity changes in the Bretton Woods structure – and in practice they took plenty of time. The German revaluation of 1961, the British devaluation of 1967, the French devaluation of 1969 and the devaluation of the dollar in 1971 had all been widely expected for a long time when they occurred, and were also widely thought to have been delayed longer than was necessary – in fact, delayed until after they became inevitable.

The Bretton Woods structure collapsed because the excess supply of dollars, which resulted from expansionary monetary policy in the United States, caused unwanted increases in the foreign exchange reserves of other countries and threatened them with 'imported inflation'. But, separately, it had become clear during the Bretton Woods period that market participants could make good profits by anticipating changes in exchange rate parities. The counterparts of those profits were the losses incurred by central banks in trying vainly to defend their parities. The typical pattern was that central banks facing pressure to devalue resisted it initially, buying their own currency in exchange for dollars at a relatively high price. Later, after more pressure had been put on them, they would throw in the towel, devalue the exchange rate, and then replenish their depleted dollar reserves by selling their own currency back again for dollars, this time at a lower price. Because these activities yielded a profit to the market, the volume of financial and intellectual resources which the market devoted to them gradually increased, capital controls notwithstanding.

Several European countries reacted to the collapse of Bretton Woods by constructing their own fixed-but-adjustable exchange rate structure, known as the 'snake in the tunnel', which was the forerunner of the ERM. The participants liked the fixed exchange rate features of Bretton Woods, but not the fact that the dollar was the key currency. The snake arrangement was attractive to them because it provided the first but not the second. Other countries concluded that they would prefer to float. By 1980, 32 IMF member countries had flexible exchange rates: there had been virtually none in 1970.

The trend towards floating was more than just a reaction against imported inflation from the United States. It was supported by a powerful current of intellectual opinion which asserted that financial markets could be relied on to manage exchange rates and that official involvement was likely to do harm rather than good. The underlying idea was that market participants – 'stabilizing speculators' – would react when the market exchange rate had diverged from its longer-term equilibrium and would have a profit incentive to act promptly so as to bring it back into line. The argument was seductive, and the idea of an autonomous national monetary policy, unconstrained by the need to maintain a fixed exchange rate parity, was very attractive.

Experience of floating in the 1970s and 1980s was not what had been hoped for. There was plenty of activity in foreign exchange markets, encouraged by the removal of direct controls on credit in many countries, by the rapid growth of euro-currency markets, and by the general retreat from capital controls and the ensuing explosive growth in international capital markets.

The 1970s were a period of high and volatile inflation, of oil price shocks, and of sudden, unpredictable policy changes. Exchange rates were volatile. In the European 'snake in the tunnel' there were numerous parity changes, which were mostly profitably anticipated by market participants. Moreover, many countries which did not have fixed exchange rates nevertheless intervened quite heavily in their foreign exchange markets to try to influence their exchange rates. Over the decade, the central banks probably lost money to position-takers in the market through this process.

Although this experience was deeply unsatisfactory, it was obvious that floating exchange rates were not the source of the problem. The source of the problem was bad domestic economic policies. Specifically, many industrial countries failed to tighten monetary policy sufficiently in the early 1970s, so that inflation rose sharply, aggravated by the oil price rises of 1973–4. In the group of industrial countries (as defined by the IMF), average consumer price inflation rose from 5.6% in 1970 to 11.5% in 1975.[28] Inflation increased in different industrial countries by different amounts. Among the countries which now comprise the G7, the *dispersion* of rates of inflation (highest rate of inflation *minus* lowest) increased from 3.3% in 1970 to 18.3% in 1975.[29] In these circumstances, it would have been quite impossible to sustain fixed exchange rates (because to do so would have required large changes in real exchange rates which were not warranted by economic fundamentals). Even within Europe, the 'snake in the tunnel' had not been a very stable arrangement. At a global level, floating exchange rates were the only possible option.

[28] IMF, *International Financial Statistics.*
[29] Ibid.

31

Foreign exchange market activity continued to grow in the 1980s and 1990s, while macroeconomic conditions in the industrialized world gradually became more stable as more and more countries came to acknowledge that there was no long-run trade-off between unemployment and inflation, and attached the highest priority to achieving low inflation. In 1979, the European Union formalized the 'snake in the tunnel' and turned it into the European Exchange Rate Mechanism, which in turn became the precursor of the single currency, the euro.

It can fairly be said that 'stabilizing speculators' – the people who were supposed to make floating exchange rates succeed – had a very difficult job in the 1970s because economic policy in many countries was so unpredictable that it was very hard to discern what the fundamentals were. It became easier in the 1980s as policy priorities became more coherent and were more clearly articulated. Nevertheless there were a number of episodes in which floating exchange rates became clearly detached from fundamentals, without there being a prompt or effective reaction from 'stabilizing speculators'. One was the collapse of the dollar in the late 1970s and the simultaneous appreciation of the Deutschmark and the Swiss franc. Another even more egregious example was the appreciation and consequent overvaluation of the dollar in the mid-1980s. In both cases it was clear after the event that huge returns could have been made by market participants willing to take positions based on a well-judged and well-timed view of the fundamentals.

Perhaps it was these episodes that encouraged the emergence of leveraged funds as foreign exchange market players.[30] Hedge funds and other institutions, such as the proprietary trading desks of investment banks, are prepared to leverage the funds provided by their proprietors, so that their power in the markets, and the risks they run, can be very large. Moreover, they have the advantage that their proprietors are generally willing to be patient and to tolerate short-term losses provided they feel confident of longer-run profits. Of course their activities were not and are not confined to foreign exchange but they have at times been a very powerful influence on foreign exchange markets.

Their power has two sources and it is important to distinguish between them. One is the power of intellect which they apply to analysing economics and markets. It is plainly highly desirable that adequate intellectual resources should be applied to the determination of such important economic variables as exchange rates. From the viewpoint of the fund manager, the application of intellectual resources can be particularly valuable where a fixed-but-adjustable exchange rate has become misaligned but the responsible monetary authorities have failed to react promptly and effectively.

[30] The first global survey of foreign exchange market turnover was conducted in 1986. Since then, surveys have been undertaken triennially – in 1989, 1992, 1995 and 1998. The results have been published by the Bank for International Settlements. They reveal very fast growth of turnover since 1989 – running consistently at a rate of growth of 11% p.a. in dollar value, much faster than the growth of international trade. To a large extent this reflected more sophisticated balance sheet management by companies, which were learning gradually how to protect themselves against wide fluctuations in exchange rates, as well as increasingly sophisticated treasury management by commercial and investment banks. But it also reflected the growing importance of hedge funds in foreign exchange.

The other source of leveraged funds' power is the sheer weight of money which they can bring to bear. At times when these funds were a dominant influence in foreign exchange, there was intense competition among intermediaries to deal with the leading funds, just in order to find out what they were doing. When a major fund took a particular position, others tended to follow, if only out of respect for the intellectual reputations of the leading fund managers. It also meant that when the leader wanted to unwind the position, other funds not only had the same position, so that they did not want to act as a counterparty, but, being followers, they wanted to unwind it too. Thus market liquidity dried up just when it was most needed, so that prices reacted unusually violently to what might have seemed a small piece of news. One good example, albeit not in foreign exchange, is the problems faced by Long-Term Capital Management in closing out loss-making positions in August and September 1998.[31] Another related example followed shortly afterwards: many fund managers had taken short positions in yen from 1995 onwards, when the yen seemed seriously overvalued and Japanese interest rates were very low. This was indeed stabilizing speculation, and it led to a much-needed depreciation of the yen. But losses on other positions, initially in

[31] See 'Hedge Funds, Leverage and the Lessons of Long-Term Capital Management', Report of the President's Working Group on Financial Markets, published by the US Department of the Treasury, Board of Governors of the Federal Reserve System, Securities and Exchange Commission, and Commodities Futures Trading Commission, April 1999. See also Report of the Financial Stability Forum Working Group on Highly Leveraged Institutions, April 2000, available at *http://www.fsforum.org/Reports/RepHLI02.pdf*.

Russia but later also in other markets after the LTCM collapse, led many of them to want to reduce their positions and take profits where they could. As a result, there was a surge of demand to buy yen which led to a violent and sudden large appreciation of the yen, causing large losses to those who had sold yen not long before that. The Federal Reserve Bank of New York's description of the episode is worth quoting at length:

At the outset of the quarter [i.e. at the beginning of October 1998], market unease regarding global financial market instability was on the rise. Although the dollar began the period at ¥136.50, it soon depreciated suddenly and sharply as hedge funds and other speculative accounts liquidated long dollar positions in an effort to reduce risk, deleverage balance sheets, and cover losses incurred in other markets. On October 7, the dollar–yen exchange rate fell 6.7 percent, from ¥133.90 to ¥120.55 – the largest percentage change in one day since 1974. Volatility in the exchange rate intensified during the following morning's New York trading session, with the dollar falling to a low of ¥111.58 but then suddenly rebounding to a high of ¥123.40. Many market participants ascribed the dollar's burst of strength to rumours of central bank intervention or market inquiries by monetary officials. Others noted that the exchange rate's rebound occurred only after the market achieved a reasonable degree of confidence that no official intervention had taken place. Still, many market participants noted persistent interest in selling dollars in the range around ¥120, largely because of concerns that levels above this range would spark a fresh round of position unwinding. The rapidity and magnitude of the price movements contributed to a decrease in direct interbank dealing, and bid–ask spreads quoted by some banks were several times wider than typical levels.[32]

As a result of their experiences, hedge funds appear (at the time of writing, at the end of 2000) to have devoted less capital to position-taking in foreign exchange markets over the past couple of years. Moreover, thanks to improvements in the technology of risk management, banks and other financial intermediaries which act as market makers are much better able to measure and contain the financial risks to which they are exposed. On top of that, the advent of electronic trading has widened access to information about market prices and made it harder for market makers to earn profits. Consequently, market makers as a group have taken less risk. Thus the risk-taking capacity of the market in general has decreased and, as a result, in the past two years or so exchange rates have become less responsive to perceived changes in fundamentals, and markets have become less liquid.

Exchange rates appear to have become driven less by fundamentals and much more by transactions. What does that mean? Some transactions are not very sensitive to the level of the exchange rate – they have to be undertaken more or less irrespective of the exchange rate level. Because they are sometimes large, and because there is a dearth of market participants willing to take a position on the other side of the transaction based on their view

[32] Federal Reserve Bank of New York, 'Treasury and Federal Reserve Foreign Exchange Operations', *Federal Reserve Bulletin*, March 1999, pp. 178–83.

of the fundamentals, the result can be that the exchange rate moves a long way, so that short-term exchange rate fluctuations can often be explained by the incidence of particular transactions. For example, a major influence on sterling in the last couple of years has been foreign exchange transactions associated with inward takeovers – takeovers of UK companies by foreign acquirers. It is not completely clear why so many inward takeovers to the United Kingdom involve foreign exchange transactions, or why outward takeovers from the United Kingdom are less likely to involve foreign exchange transactions, but it appears to be the case nonetheless. Thus the increased risk aversion of market participants may have had its private virtues, but it will also have had public costs if, as seems likely, one of its side-effects is that, on average, exchange rates now diverge from their fundamental values by more than in the past.

It is clear from the above that the microeconomic nature of the foreign exchange market is not something that can be regarded as constant and unchanging for the purposes of interpreting exchange rate fluctuations. In fact, the behaviour patterns of the market have changed substantially over the past decades, partly in response to changes in the behaviour of central banks. Because the microeconomic nature and behaviour patterns of the market are important and subject to change, it is important for central banks to monitor them closely, and this is one of the reasons why most central banks maintain a presence in the foreign exchange market, even if their exchange rates are floating.

(c) The choice of exchange rate regime

After the collapse of Bretton Woods, many countries saw floating exchange rates as a protection from the unwanted volatility caused by monetary policy changes in the United States. However, some countries acknowledged that benefit then – and more do so now – but they were concerned that the foreign exchange market itself could be an independent source of unwanted volatility. Thus they reject the view that the foreign exchange market is an efficient organism that can be relied on to price the currency on the basis of the fundamentals, but implicitly go along with the point of view, based on the experience of the 1920s and 1930s, that led to the introduction of fixed-but-adjustable exchange rate parities as a key feature of Bretton Woods. More recently, John Williamson has asserted that the major drawback of freely floating exchange rates is

> that the capricious variation in freely floating exchange rates results not just in short-run volatility, which may be a nuisance but can effectively be hedged through forward markets, but also in long-run misalignments, which can be highly disruptive of good economic performance.[33]

Is the foreign exchange market an independent source of volatility? An answer to the question requires a comparison of the actual behaviour pattern of exchange rates with a hypothetical behaviour pattern based on the assumption that foreign exchange markets are not an independent

[33] John Williamson, *Exchange Rate Regimes for Emerging Markets: Reviving the Intermediate Option* (Washington, DC: Institute for International Economics, 2000).

source of volatility. If that assumption were warranted, rate fluctuations would be explicable *ex post* by fluctuations in economic fundamentals. Tests of whether exchange rate fluctuations can be explained *ex post* by fluctuations in economic fundamentals have generally yielded negative results.[34] For example, in 1983 Richard Meese and Kenneth Rogoff,[35] examining the behaviour of the dollar/pound, dollar/mark, dollar/yen and trade-weighted dollar rates in the 1970s, concluded that the nihilistic random walk model performs as well in out-of-sample forecasting as any of a range of estimated models based on fundamentals. Empirical work since 1983, even though it has been able to use more recent data from a period of greater macroeconomic stability, has not produced very different results. Thus Robert Flood and Andrew Rose, writing in 1999, comment that:

> Simply put, to a first approximation countries with fixed exchange rates have less volatile exchange rates than floating countries, but macroeconomies that are equally volatile.
>
> This stylised fact is inconsistent with theories that model either the exchange rate or the exchange rate regime as manifestations of underlying economic shocks. Unsurprisingly, such theories have performed poorly when applied to the data. Neither the exchange rate nor the exchange rate regime seems to reflect observable economic shocks. There are exceptions – countries with high inflation – and the theories do

[34] Though such tests are always vulnerable to the accusation that they have looked at the wrong fundamentals.
[35] R. P. Meese and K. Rogoff, 'Empirical Exchange Rate Models of the Seventies: Do They Fit Out of Sample?', *Journal of International Economics*, Vol. 14 (1983).

work better at long horizons. But at short and medium frequencies, the exchange rates of low-inflation countries are almost unrelated to macroeconomic phenomena.[36]

If economic models cannot explain fluctuations in the exchange rates even of large industrial countries in terms of fundamentals, then the view that the foreign exchange market can be a source of instability has some plausibility, particularly in countries where the market is small and thin, and where the private sector does not devote many resources to analysing the fundamentals.[37]

Some central bankers certainly do think that the foreign exchange market is an independent source of volatility. To quote Ian Macfarlane, Governor of the Reserve Bank of Australia:

Our whole approach to foreign exchange intervention is based on our view that the foreign exchange market is not 'efficient' in the academic sense, but that it is prone to overshooting in both directions from time to time.[38]

[36] R. P. Flood and A. K. Rose, 'Understanding Exchange Rate Volatility', *Economic Journal*, Vol. 109, November 1999, pp. F660–72. See also R. P. Flood and A. K. Rose, 'Fixing Exchange Rates: A Virtual Quest for Fundamentals', *Journal of Monetary Economics*, Vol. 36, 1995, pp. 3–37, and K. Rogoff, 'Monetary Models of Dollar/Yen/Euro Nominal Exchange Rates: Dead or Undead?', *Economic Journal*, Vol. 109, November 1999, pp. F655–9.
[37] Financial market dynamics in small and medium-sized open economies, and the role of highly leveraged institutions, are discussed in the Report of the Financial Stability Forum Working Group on Highly Leveraged Institutions (see note 31 above).
[38] I. J. Macfarlane, 'Recent International Developments in Perspective', Address to the CEDA Annual General Meeting, Melbourne, 25 November 1998; reprinted in *Reserve Bank of Australia Bulletin*, December 1998.

And Sushil Wadhwani, a member of the Bank of England Monetary Policy Committee, recently commented that:

> the fact that the euro has, sometimes, failed to respond to news about structural reform in Euroland does suggest that it has, to some extent, acquired a 'life of its own'.[39]

For monetary authorities which take this view of the foreign exchange market, the choice of exchange rate regime involves some kind of trade-off between the benefits of monetary policy autonomy and the costs of market-induced exchange rate volatility. And where the choice is a floating exchange rate, there are reasons to look for ways of limiting volatility in the rate without surrendering monetary autonomy.

Those ways include holding foreign exchange reserves which can be used to support the currency in case of need. As evidence of this, consider the group of 25 countries which had floating exchange rates in both 1990 and 1999. The foreign exchange reserves of that group of countries grew substantially faster during the 1990s than the total of global foreign exchange reserves: their share of global reserves rose from 32% to 37%. This demonstrates rather starkly that countries with floating exchange rates do not necessarily wish to accept the exchange rate determined by the market, and think that they may be able to influence the exchange rate by intervening in the foreign exchange market. Of course, if

[39] Sushil Wadhwani, 'The Exchange Rate and the MPC: What Can We Do?', Speech delivered to the Senior Business Forum at the Centre for Economic Performance on 31 May 2000.

41

reserves are to be useful for this purpose, they need to be accessible at short notice, and not committed to investments which cannot readily be turned into cash. It is also important that the reserves are not hypothecated against the servicing of external liabilities. It is notable and welcome that international guidelines on reserve management and debt management stress these important points.

Also, as mentioned above, defence mechanisms against market-induced exchange rate volatility include controls on capital flows, particularly short-term flows, though there is not much evidence on their costs and benefits.

It has been suggested that, as markets have become more efficient, the only viable exchange rate regimes are 'corner solutions' – that is, either absolute fixity, for example, dollarization, or a currency board, or a monetary union; or else floating. On that view, 'fixed-but-adjustable' exchange rates are unsustainable. Evidence in support of that view is that in 1999, nearly two-thirds of IMF member countries had adopted a corner solution. Nevertheless, one-third had not done so. Many of them had greatly widened the band within which the exchange rate is allowed to fluctuate: for example, the fluctuation bands in ERM2[40] are 15% either side of parity. In this way they greatly reduce the risk of needing to intervene to defend the parity. I suggest that at least in some cases, their reasons for not abandoning the parity completely

[40] The post-single currency version of the European Exchange Rate Mechanism, intended as a transitional regime for countries aspiring to join the single currency.

include the belief that in the absence of much private-sector analysis of the fundamentals, the official parity still provides some useful guidance to the market.

As noted above, the debate about fixed and floating exchange rates is continuing, unabated and unsettled, after many decades. Practice is continuing to evolve, too. Of the 43 countries which had floating exchange rates in 1990, only 25 still had them in 1999. This changeability no doubt reflects both the difficulty of resolving the issues and the ever-changing microeconomics of the foreign exchange market.

4 CONCLUSION

The integration of the world economy through international capital movements has become closer since the 1960s, but not as much closer as might have been expected after the explosive growth in financial intermediation since the 1970s. Even in the 1990s, capital seems to have been much less mobile internationally than it was in the era of the gold standard in the late nineteenth and early twentieth centuries.

There are several categories of reason for the less-than-complete integration. Official controls on capital flows have played a role, and although they remain in some countries, they are much less pervasive than in the 1960s and 1970s and they are mainly aimed at short-term flows. There are cultural and legal obstacles to international capital flows, and a continuing tension in many countries between domestic cultural sentiment and the interests of globalization; in recent years, however, the interests of globalization seem to have been gaining ground as its benefits have become more apparent.

Nevertheless, fears of monetary and financial instability remain an important obstacle to international capital flows. The choice of exchange rate regime remains for many countries an unsolved problem, and the choices that countries actually make change surprisingly often. While floating exchange rates offer the reward of monetary policy autonomy, many fear that they also bring with them a degree of market-induced volatility.

Discussion of exchange rate policies has tended too readily to neglect the microeconomic nature and behaviour patterns of the foreign exchange market, even though they have been subject to substantial change since floating exchange rates became widespread in the 1970s. This neglect may help to explain the failure of models based on macroeconomic fundamentals to explain exchange rate fluctuations *ex post*.

In a sense, the analytical error of the models has perhaps been to assume too readily that markets have been in a stable equilibrium.[41] For sure, the foreign exchange markets have been continuously in a series of temporary equilibria. But it is far from clear that they have yet reached any kind of longer-term equilibrium. The supply of capital devoted to 'stabilizing speculation' in foreign exchange appears to have been very variable, and the variations have had important effects on market behaviour. Because 'stabilizing speculation' is supposed to play a crucial role in the functioning of flexible exchange rates, it is hardly surprising that debates on exchange rate regimes remain unsettled and that countries change their minds about exchange rate regimes as often as they do.

---

[41] This is the conclusion reached by Flood and Rose, 'Understanding Exchange Rate Volatility' (see note 36 above).

APPENDIX: THE ESTIMATION OF INTERNATIONAL CAPITAL MOBILITY

The data set is taken from the *OECD Statistical Compendium 2000–01*, available on CD-ROM. It incorporates annual current-price data on GDP, private and government consumption (PC and GC respectively), and fixed investment and stockbuilding (FI and SB respectively) for the following 29 countries:

Australia	1960–97	Luxembourg	1960–97
Austria	1960–97	Mexico	1960–97
Belgium	1960–97	Netherlands	1960–97
Canada	1960–97	New Zealand	1960–97
Czech Republic	1990–97	Norway	1960–97
Denmark	1960–97	Poland	1990–97
Finland	1960–97	Portugal	1960–97
France	1960–97	South Korea	1970–97
Germany*	1960–97	Spain	1960–97
Greece	1960–97	Sweden	1960–97
Hungary	1990–97	Switzerland	1960–97
Iceland	1960–97	Turkey	1960–97
Ireland	1960–97	UK	1960–97
Italy	1960–97	USA	1960–97
Japan	1960–97		

* For 1960–90, I used data for West Germany; for 1991 onwards I used data for the whole of Germany.

The percentage savings ratio I calculated for each country in each year as

$$S = 100 * (GDP-PC-GC)/GDP$$

and the investment ratio as

$$I = 100 * (FI+ SB)/GDP$$

I then calculated average savings and investment ratios for each country over the four longer periods 1960–69, 1970–79, 1980–89 and 1990–97. The figures quoted in Table 1 are cross-country correlation coefficients between savings and investment ratios, one for each of the four longer periods. To give a specific example, the correlation coefficient quoted for the 1960s is calculated as

$$\frac{\sum_{j}\left(s_{j}(1960s)-\bar{s}(1960s)\right)\left(i_{j}(1960s)-\bar{i}(1960s)\right)}{\sqrt{\sum_{j}\left(s_{j}(1960s)-\bar{s}(1960s)\right)^{2}}\sqrt{\sum_{j}\left(i_{j}(1960s)-\bar{i}(1960s)\right)^{2}}}$$

where $s_{j}(1960s)$ and $i_{j}(1960s)$ are the average savings and investment ratios, respectively of country j in 1960–69 and $\bar{s}(1960s)$ and $\bar{i}(1960s)$ are the cross-section average of country averages of savings and investment ratios in 1960–69.